Mermaids in Wonderland

A Coloring and Puzzle-Solving Adventure for All Ages

Illustrations
and Text
by Marcos Chin

HARPER
DESIGN
An Imprint of HarperCollins Publishers

There are five gifts waiting for you in Wonderland. Find them by locating the correct number of magical lettered keys hidden within the five groups of drawings on the following pages. Collect all the keys and unscramble the letters to solve the riddle to collect the gift that will help you on the next leg of your journey.

It's time to put on your magical fins,
start your coloring journey,
and find gifts as you swim.

Find five keys in this group of drawings to find the answer on page 25.

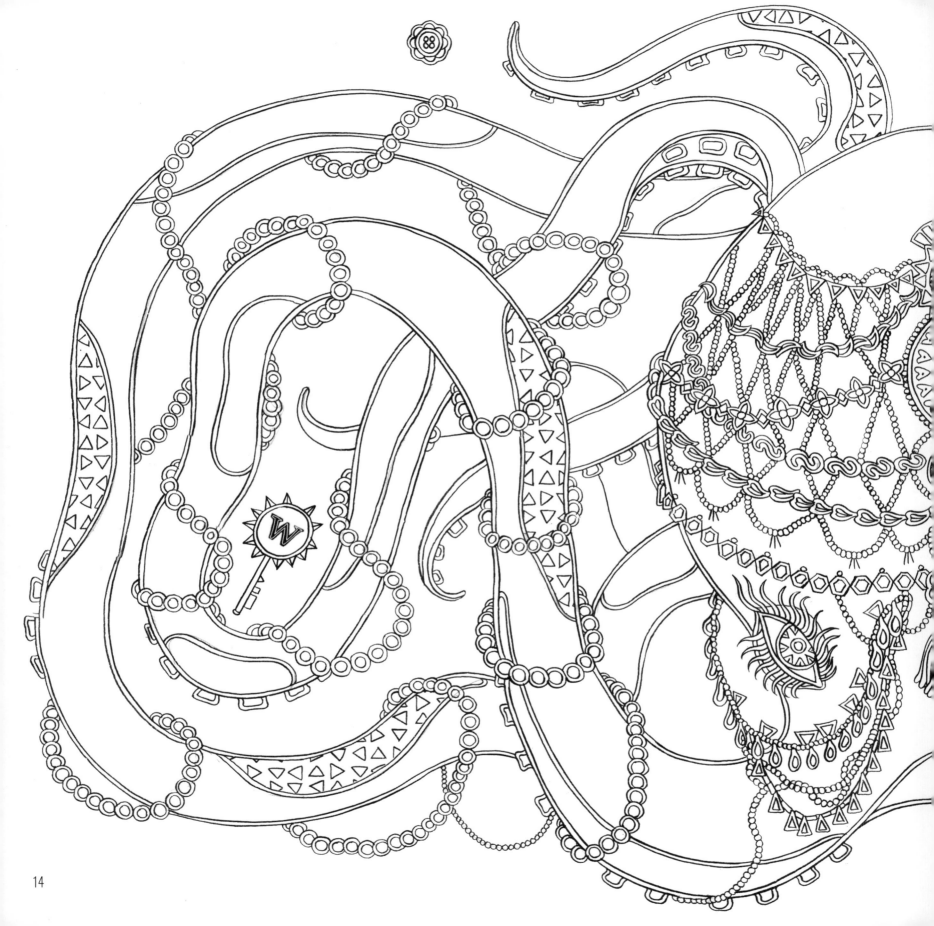

24

Float like a butterfly, sting like a bee—
Neither creature could exist without me.
I may help a chicken flee the coop
Or lift a daredevil in a loopity-loop.
Made of wax, I'll melt as sunrise is sure.
Made of metal, I'll go on a worldwide tour.

What am I?

The letters of the five keys hold the answer.

Wear these WINGS to help you fly out of the Wonderland waters and find four keys to answer the riddle on page 39.

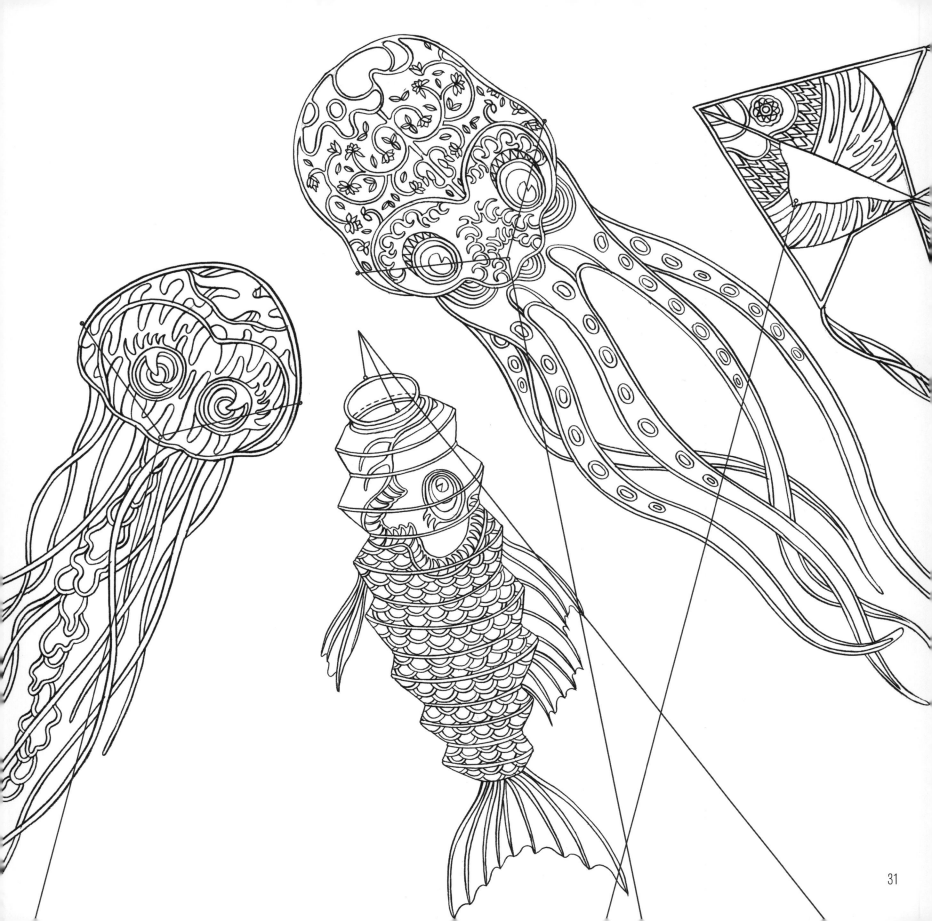

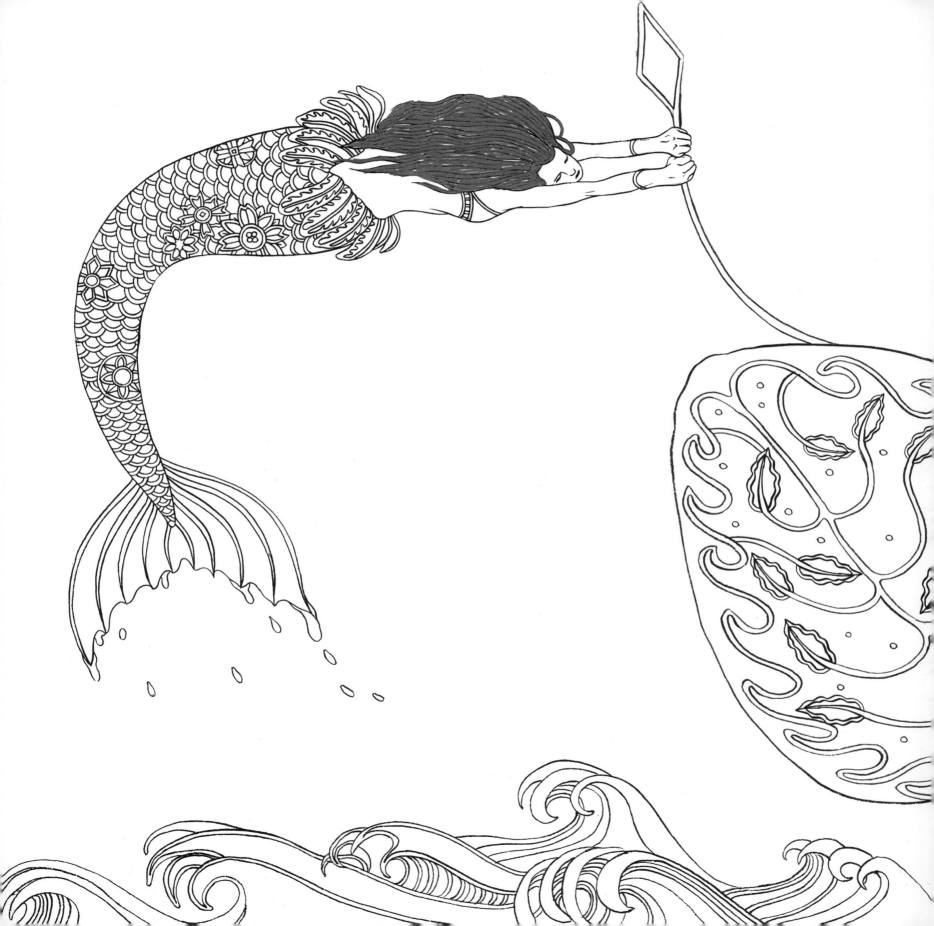

Shiny and round, I have two faces,
And I may look different in foreign places.
I have no mouth and make no sound
Until dropped into a slot or on hard ground.

What am I?

The letters of the four keys hold the answer.

Use the magic COIN to grant you access to the Wonderland sea park and then look for the four keys that form the answer to the riddle on page 55.

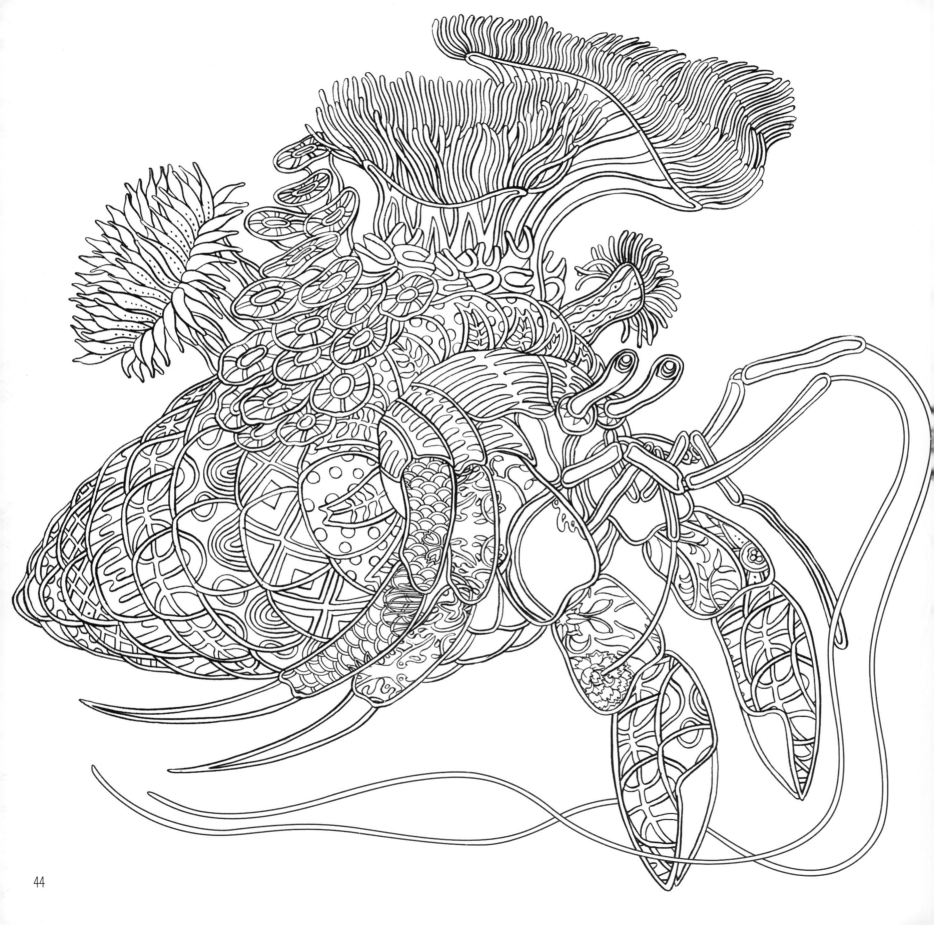

I can make a heart sing,
Though I am not a symphony,
And most women are glad when
    I come from Tiffany.
I lack a beginning and an end,
I symbolize promise, a forever friend.

What am I?

The letters of the four keys hold the answer.

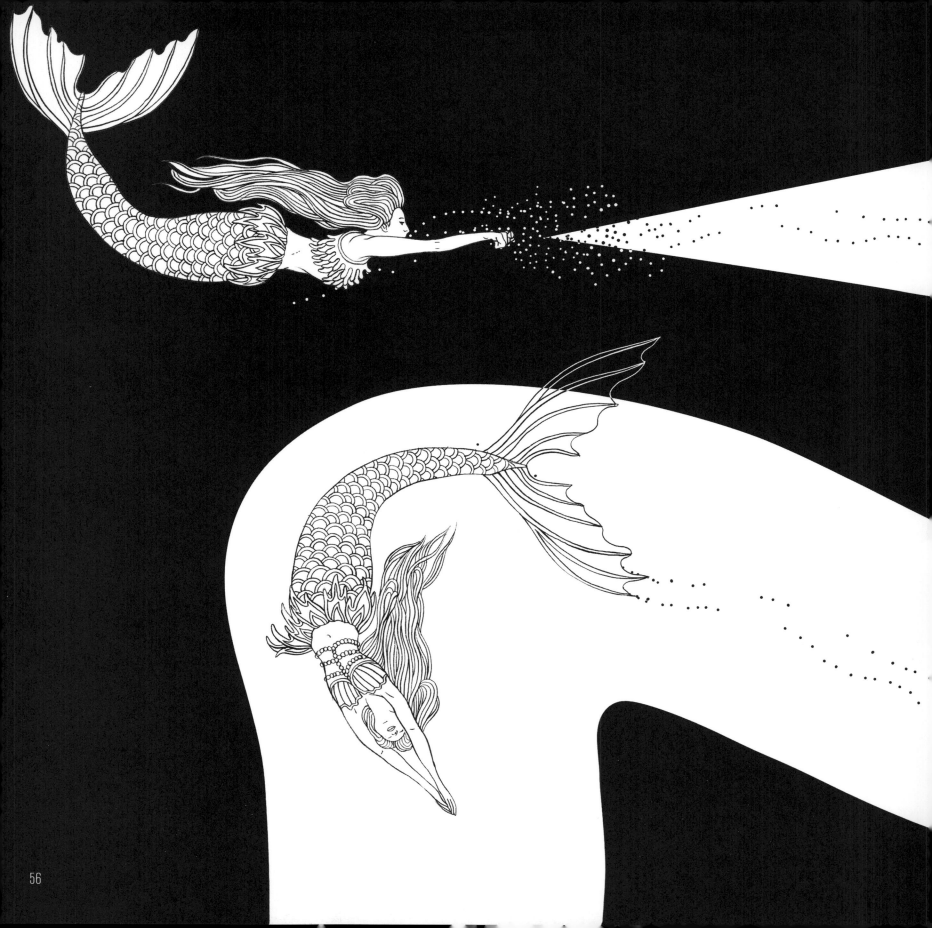

As you swim deeper into the Wonderland sea, use the light from the magic RING to guide you through the darkness and find the six keys that form the answer to the riddle on page 75.

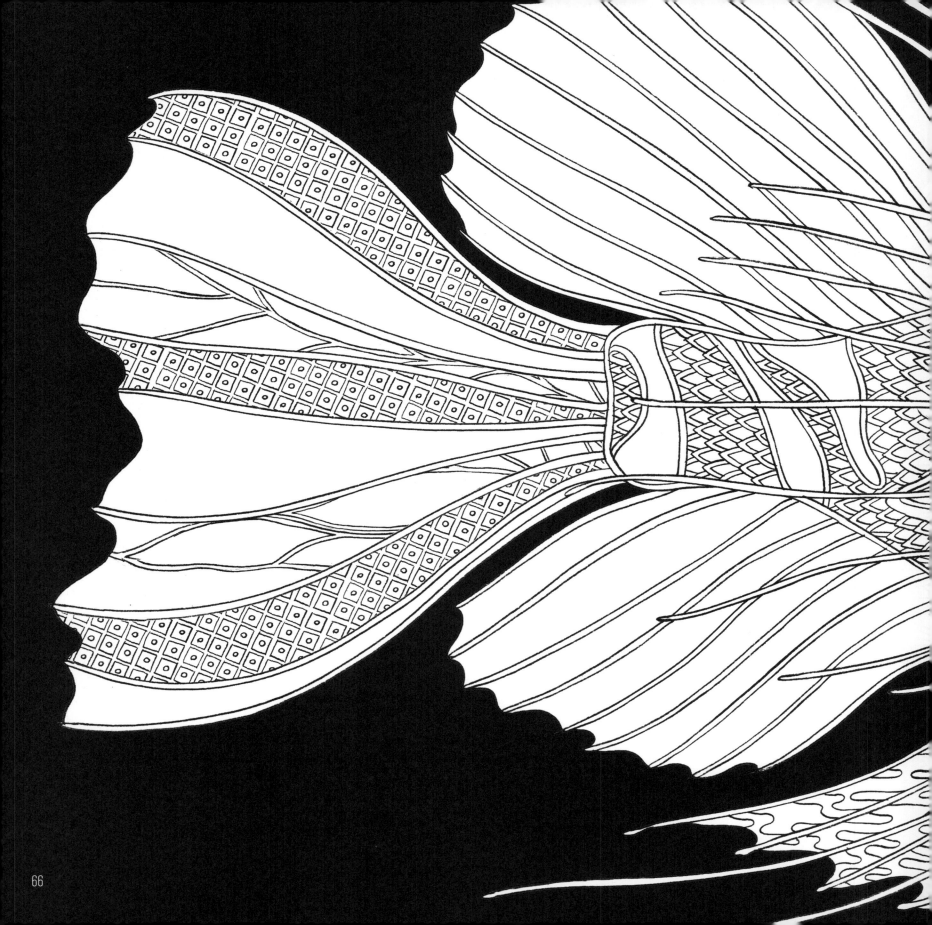

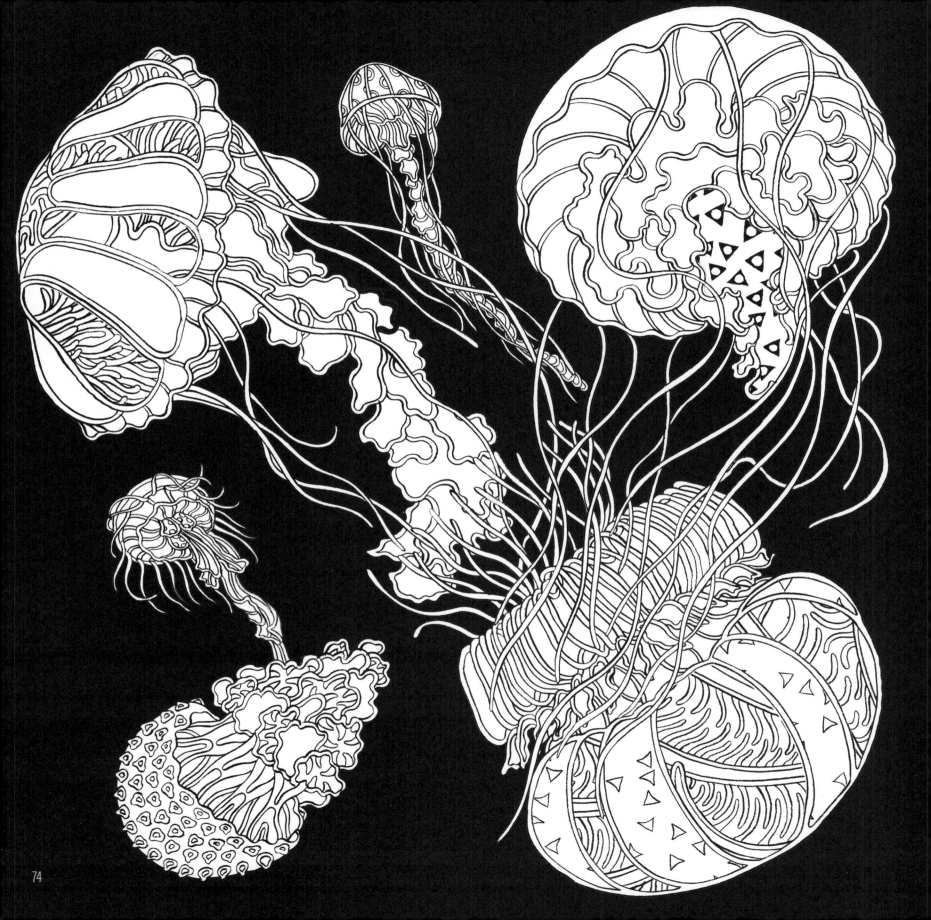

A Wicked Queen once asked me,
"Who is the most fair?"
And to reply to her honestly,
I certainly did dare.
While I see all through and through
What you see in me is up to you.

What am I?

The letters of the six keys hold the answer.

Use the MIRROR to put scary sea creatures to sleep to allow you safe passage through the dark Wonderland waters as you search for the six new keys that form the answer to the riddle on page 91.

I'm mightier than a sword,
But I weigh a lot less.
You might opt to use me
When you have thoughts to express.
I work in the water,
That you'll soon see.
Solve this last riddle,
And I'll help set you free.

What am I?

The letters of the six keys hold the answer.

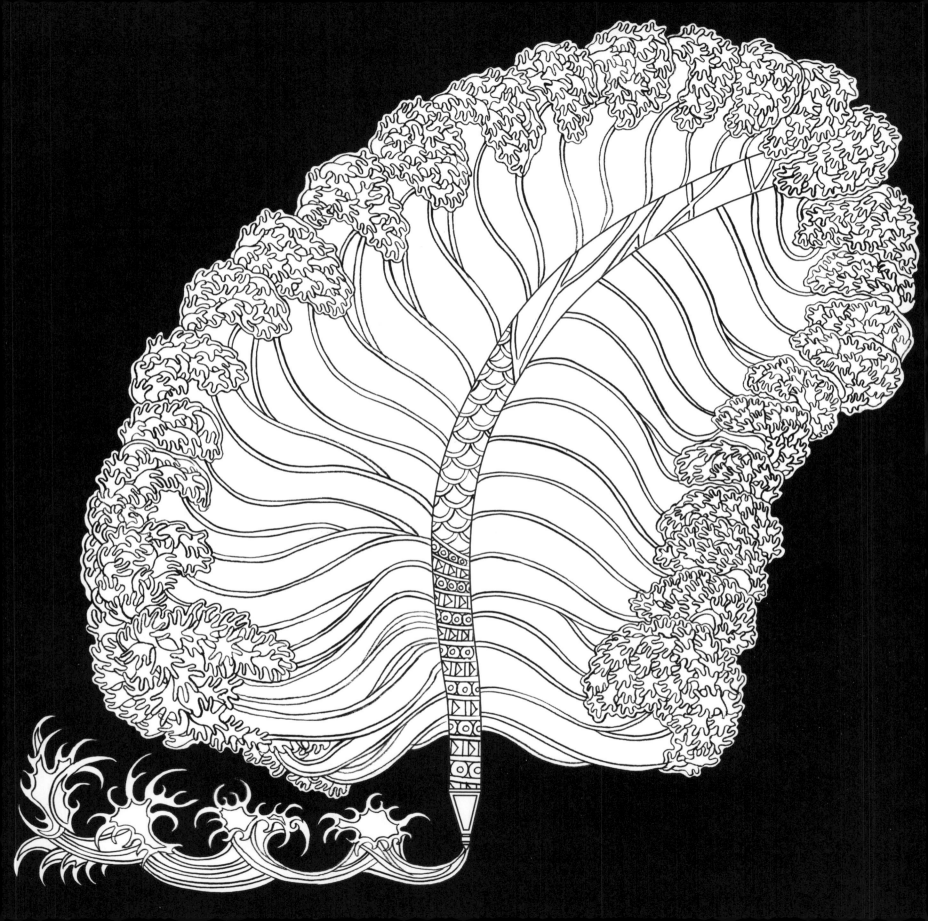

Use the magical SEA PEN to guide you through the maze to reach the secret door that leads you out of Wonderland.

Mermaids in Wonderland

Text and illustrations © 2017 by Marcos Chin

HarperCollins books may be purchased for educational, business, or sales promotional use. For information please e-mail the Special Markets Department at SPsales@harpercollins.com.

First published in 2017 by
Harper Design
An Imprint of HarperCollins*Publishers*
195 Broadway
New York, NY 10007
Tel: (212) 207-7000
Fax: (855) 746-6023
harperdesign@harpercollins.com
www.hc.com

Distributed throughout the world by
HarperCollins*Publisher*s
195 Broadway
New York, NY 10007

ISBN 978-0-06-246560-3

Library of Congress Control Number: 2015953149

Book design by Nancy Leonard

Printed in China

First Printing, 2017

About the Illustrator

Marcos Chin is an award-winning illustrator whose work has appeared on book and CD covers, in advertisements, fashion catalogs, surface and textile designs, and magazines. The author and illustrator of the bestselling *Fairies in Wonderland: An Interactive Coloring Adventure for All Ages* (Harper Design, 2016), he also created the illustrations for the children's book *Ella*, by Mallory Kasdan. He has worked with HBO, Neiman Marcus, MTA Arts for Transit, Fiat, *Time*, *Rolling Stone*, *The New Yorker*, *GQ*, and the *New York Times*. In 2013 his illustration "Grand Central Catwalk" appeared in New York City subways, celebrating Grand Central Terminal's centennial year. Chin lectures and gives workshops on illustration throughout the United States and abroad, and also teaches at the School of Visual Arts in New York City. He lives in Brooklyn, New York. **www.marcoschin.com**